MEN-AT-ARMS SERIES

EDITOR: MARTIN WINDROW

The Australian Army at War 1899-1975

Text by JOHN LAFFIN

Colour plates by MIKE CHAPPELL

D1294845

OSPREY PUBLISHING LONDON

Published in 1982 by
Osprey Publishing Ltd
Member company of the George Philip Group
12–14 Long Acre, London WC2E 9LP
© Copyright 1982 Osprey Publishing Ltd

ISBN 0 85045 418 2

Filmset in Great Britain
Printed in Hong Kong

The Seeds of Legend

The British public got their first look at Australian troops in 1897 when 37 men of the New South Wales Lancers attended Queen Victoria's Diamond Jubilee. Officers from Britain and all over the Empire were impressed with the lancers' horsemanship, which won them two of the five gold medals awarded for competition in tournaments among regular, territorial and colonial mounted troops from throughout the Empire.

The British people were to get many further views of the Australians, on parade or through the newspapers and later by means of film and television. They have had a brief military history, by world standards, but they have taken part in nine wars and, British troops apart, they have fought in more countries than the soldiers of any other nation. Friend and foe alike have assessed them as men-at-arms perhaps equalled but never surpassed. In many ways they are certainly different. . . .

Australian soldiers of all wars since 1914–18 have been called 'Anzacs' from the initial letters of Australian and New Zealand Army Corps. (In Army slang there is also an 'Anzac button' – a nail used in place of a button; and 'Anzac stew', – an urn of hot water in which floats one bacon rind!) C. E. W. Bean, the Australian official historian of the First World War, gave the word Anzac its most expressive meaning: it stood, he said, for 'reckless valour and a good cause, for enterprise, resourcefulness, fidelity, comradeship and mateship'.

The word 'Digger' has a much stronger connection with Australian soldiers than with New Zealanders, though it was probably in use in 1916 among both Australians and New Zealanders, and it was common in 1917. Bean said that the word evolved from the professional gum-diggers

of New Zealand. Many old soldiers believed that it came about as a natural result of their trench-digging in France and Flanders; others claim that some West Australian soldiers, gold-diggers in civil life, started the word on its way. At one time it was the slang expression for a plodder – an apt term for an infantryman.

A rare photograph of Lt. Harry Morant, 'The Breaker', taken in Adelaide shortly before he sailed for South Africa with the Second Contingent of the South Australian Mounted Rifles. After this tour of duty Morant went to England, but returned to South Africa to join the Bush Veldt Carbineers; and it was while serving with this unit that he is alleged to have murdered Boer prisoners, the 'crime' for which he was condemned by a blatantly unsound court martial, and executed by firing squad in Pretoria on 27 February 1902. The recent and critically acclaimed feature film 'Breaker Morant', starring Edward Woodward, is a fairly accurate account of Morant's second tour of duty.

South Africa 1899-1902

At the beginning of 1899 any future for the Australians as soldiers seemed remote; but Australians were soon watching with interest the growing tension between Britain and the South African Republic. As early as July 1899 the government of Queensland offered a contingent of 250 mounted infantry with machine guns, should war be declared. On 28 September, anticipating the inevitable, the various State military commandants met in Melbourne and decided to raise a joint all-arms contingent of 2,500 men, of whom more than half would be mounted. War was declared on 11 October.

The War Office accepted the Australian offer as a gesture of Imperial unity rather than as a serious military contribution; and the War Minister, Lord Landsdowne, wanted changes of emphasis. In a cable he said: 'Units should consist of 124 men, and may be infantry, mounted infantry or cavalry. . . . Infantry most, cavalry least serviceable.'

Considering that so many Australians were born to the saddle and accustomed to riding in conditions very similar to those in South Africa, Landsdowne's qualification was short-sighted. Most 'Citizen Bushmen' contingents were equipped by public subscription and, though untrained, were officered by men with previous military experience.

The standards set for enlistment for service in the South African War were published in the press and in the State gazettes: 'Men to be good shots and proficient swordsmen, of superior physique, not under 5 foot 6 inches or 34 inches chest; good riders and bushmen, accustomed to find their way about in strange country.'

In the end all Australian infantry was mounted, providing the Commander-in-Chief, Lord Roberts, with nearly double the number of mounted troops previously at his disposal; this enabled the wide flanking movements which were the determining factor in the relief of Kimberley and the advance on Bloemfontein and Pretoria.

Men of the New South Wales Mounted Rifles, 1899. The khaki jacket, trimmed with red braid and with red shoulder straps, is worn with pale Bedford cord breeches, ankle boots with four-buckle knee-length leather gaiters, and a khaki slouch hat decorated with a red puggaree and emu feathers. A canteen is slung on the right hip, a folded haversack on the left, beneath the leather waist belt and bandolier. The long socket bayonet for the Martini-Henry rifle is frogged on the left hip.

Sergeant-Major of the NSW Mounted Rifles; note the regiment's unique sword frog arrangement, and cf. Plate A2.

The first notable action in which the Australians were engaged was fought soon after the arrival of the Queensland Mounted Infantry late in 1899. On New Year's Day 1900 they took part in an attack on Boer positions at Sunnyside. Stalking the Boers in the same way that the Boers had stalked and outwitted the British, the Queens-landers advanced on three sides in an outflanking movement, captured the laager and took 40 prisoners. It was an unheard-of feat.

The first real Australian battle honour was the fight near Brakfontein on Elands River. In mid-

Australian sniper in a trench at Gallipoli, with his 'spotter' close by. The periscope rifle was invented at 'Anzac' by L/Cpl. W. Beech of the 2nd Bn. The conditions in the trenches made any standard uniform impossible. Some men wore waist-belt ammunition pouches, others bandoliers. Steel helmets were not general issue at that time. The heat in the trenches was intense; note the apathetic listlessness of the seated soldiers. (Australian War Memorial)

July 1900 Col. Hore was posted at a crossing on the river to keep it secure and open. He occupied five acres and his 'garrison' consisted of 100 men of the Queensland Mounted Infantry (Maj. Tunbridge), 100 of New South Wales Bushmen (Capt. Thomas) and 50 Victorian Bushmen (Capt. Ham).

The Australian post was on a flat plain near a boulder-covered hill which commanded not only the Australians but the nearest point of the river, half a mile away. By August up to 4,000 Boers with nine field guns surrounded the Australians' five acres. On 4 August the Boer guns fired 1,500 shells into the defensive perimeter, killing five men and wounding 27. The horses suffered terribly; of the 1,540 in camp, 1,379 were lost. By night the Australians used timber from smashed wagons to roof their trenches; they brought water from the river, and relieved their forward posts. During the darkness the Boers used a 'pom-pom' quick-firer which irritated the Australians. Lieut. Amant, a young Queenslander, took 25 men, raided the Boer post, killed the crew and wrecked the gun. It was an act that was to become typical of Australian soldiers.

The Boers blocked two British relief forces, and their leader, Delarey, sent in a message inviting Hore to surrender or be blown to pieces. Hore replied that even if he personally wanted to surrender he was in command of Australians who would cut his throat if he did. The Australians dominated the battlefied at night. They wiped out several gun crews by creeping close and firing at the flashes. Boers who tried to infiltrate were outplayed at their own game; Australian forward scouts and listening posts of two or three men killed and routed far stronger enemy patrols. Even by day the Australians, without permission, went out stalking snipers.

The morning of 16 August was oddly quiet at Elands River. Reconnaissance patrols found that the Boers had abandoned their posts; even the guns had been taken away. Later that day a relief force led by Lord Kitchener rode into Elands River. Kitchener told the defenders: 'You have had a hot time but have made a remarkable defence. Only Colonials could have held out and survived in such impossible circumstances.' Great praise came from a Boer historian. 'For the first time in the war we were fighting men who used our own tactics against us. They were Australian volunteers and . . . we could not take their positions. They were the only troops who could scout into our lines at night and kill our sentries, while killing or capturing our scouts. . . . The Australians were formidable opponents.'

On 1 January 1901 the Federation of Australian States came into effect; that is, for the first time there was a nation rather than a country called Australia. This changed the status of the various State contingents; welded together, they were designated Australian Commonwealth Horse. At the time of Federation the various State forces comprised Permanent troops (paid and full-time), Militia (paid and part-time) and Volunteers (unpaid and part-time). The permanent forces consisted largely of administrative staff and garrison artillery.

The States and the Commonwealth together contributed 57 contingents totalling 16,175 men, including 838 officers, to serve in the Boer War. More than 500 were killed or died of illness, and six Victoria Crosses were awarded. Australia had shown its capacity to provide willing and enthusiastic soldiers; the mounted men in particular were noted for their dash, initiative and courage and they left a lasting impression on some British leaders. The Commander-in-Chief, Lord Roberts, so admired the organisation and efficiency of the New South Wales Field Ambulance

Corps that he recommended it as a pattern for the British Army. An officer of the Corps, Capt. Neville Howse, was the first Australian to win the Victoria Cross – at Vradesort in July 1900.

While many Australians had been busy in South Africa, a smaller party – 460 volunteers – had been sent to China in 1901 to fight the Boxer rebels. Victorian members of the contingent served at Tientsin and the NSW contingent at Peking.

Capt. Phil Fry of the 10th Australian Light Horse (Western Australia) in a Gallipoli trench. Mounted action was out of the question at Gallipoli, so there is nothing noticeably 'cavalry' about the uniform. Fry wears a leather belt set, but webbing was more common. This popular officer was killed in a successful charge at Hill 60 on 29 August 1915. (Bill Connell Collection)

Pre-1914 Training

Co-ordination of a national defence effort had been one of the reasons for Federation, and one of the first actions of the new Commonwealth Parliament was to create a national Department of Defence. On 1 March 1901 all the various State forces came under the department's control and its soldiers under the command of the first GOC, Maj. Gen. Sir Edward Hutton. His aim was to make the new Army uniquely Australian in character and outlook.

Mounted troops were divided into two categories. The first comprised horsemen trained to scout, skirmish, and reconnoitre and also to fight on foot – Light Horse. The second group were infantry soldiers provided with individual four-legged transport – Mounted Infantry. The Mounted Service Manual published in 1902 was explicit about these units' rôles:

1. Light Horse are required to:
   a. Fight on foot both in the offensive and defensive.

Drawing of a Gallipoli infantryman by David Barker, himself an Anzac in 1915.

" AT THE LANDING, AND HERE EVER SINCE "

Drawn in Blue and Red Pencil by DAVID BARKER

   b. To perform the duties classed under 'Information' viz. reconnoitring and screening.
   c. Afford protection from surprise for all bodies of troops both halted and on the march.
2. Mounted infantry are required to perform only the duties pertaining to infantry and are temporarily provided with increased means of mobility.

From the beginning it was seen as important that the mounted soldier should be associated with the civil community. In 1909 Lord Kitchener was invited to assess progress and to comment on the new Army's 'adequacy'. Kitchener, though generally impressed, made many suggestions, including a citizen army of 80,000. He also recommended a Royal Military College, and this came into being in 1911 at Duntroon, Canberra. It was to provide Australia with its own trained headquarters staff and area officers for both the regular and citizen armies. The first commandant was Brig. Gen. William Bridges. Duntroon had 147 cadets when Bridges left in May 1914, and by the end of the year 71 of them were on active service; of these, 17 lost their lives at Gallipoli and 34 were wounded. Bridges was to die there with the cadets he had trained.

Kitchener's report had inspired the Defence Act of 1909, and a programme of universal military training was decreed in 1911. Also at Kitchener's suggestion, a small arms factory was opened in 1912 at Lithgow, west of Sydney, and most small arms carried by Australian troops since then have been made at Lithgow.

By 1914 the emphasis, in quality at least, was on cavalry, and in that year Australia had 23 regiments of Light Horse, a total of 9,000 superlative riders of all ranks. A regiment of Light Horse had four squadrons, each under a major, at full strength.

Throughout Australia there was a serious approach to military training, almost as if war was expected.

The Diggers 1914-18

When Australia heard the news of Britain's declaration of war against Germany in August 1914 the Prime Minister, Andrew Fisher, pledged Australia's support – 'to the last man and the last shilling'. Fisher's confidence that Australians would support him was justified. The recruiting of the initial force of 20,000 men was a triumph of staff organisation and individual ardour.

The first major decision was whether the required forces would come from the existing militia units or whether an entirely new army would be formed for the duration of hostilities. The provisions of the Kitchener Report were still being implemented and by 1914 90 per cent of the militia of 45,000 were boys of 19–21 years of age. Nobody was happy about sending a 'boys' army' overseas. So an army was raised to become a parallel organisation to the existing Australian Military Forces, with its own rates of pay, establishment and seniority list. The Commander, Maj. Gen. Bridges, had firm views about its designation. 'I want a name that will sound well when they call us by our initials. That's how they will speak of us.' In this way the Australian Imperial Force (AIF) was written into history.

Into the staging camps of each State hurried young men – though one in five was over the age of 31 – from town and country alike: clerks, bankers, solicitors and shop assistants, drovers, shearers and boundary riders. General Bridges formed them into a Light Horse Brigade and the 1st Infantry Division. These men left for Egypt on 1 November 1914. Meanwhile a force of 2,000 had landed on New Britain and accepted the surrender of German New Guinea. These troops, the Australian Naval and Military Expeditionary Force (ANMEF), remained there throughout the war.

The 1st Australian Division commenced its training in Cairo and was joined in January 1915 by the 2nd Light Horse Brigade. Brig. Gen. Harry Chauvel, commander of the 1st Light Horse Brigade, took over all the horsemen, and implanted discipline and bearing. Infantry and cavalry alike were issued with the Lithgow-made

Order of Battle
Australian Imperial Force 1914–18

1st Division
1st Bde.: 1st, 2nd, 3rd, 4th Bns.
2nd Bde.: 5th, 6th, 7th, 8th Bns.
3rd Bde.: 9th, 10th, 11th, 12th Bns.

2nd Division
5th Bde.: 17th, 18th, 19th, 20th Bns.
6th Bde.: 21st, 22nd, 23rd, 24th Bns.
7th Bde.: 25th, 26th, 27th, 28th Bns.

3rd Division
9th Bde.: 33rd, 34th, 35th, 36th Bns.
10th Bde.: 37th, 38th, 39th, 40th Bns.
11th Bde.: 41st, 42nd, 43rd, 44th Bns.

4th Division
4th Bde.: 13th, 14th, 15th, 16th Bns.
12th Bde.: 45th, 46th, 47th, 48th Bns.
13th Bde.: 49th, 50th, 51st, 52nd Bns.

5th Division
14th Bde.: 3rd, 54th, 55th, 56th Bns.
15th Bde.: 57th, 58th, 59th, 60th Bns.
8th Bde.: 29th, 30th, 31st, 32nd Bns.

Each division had its own field artillery, trench mortar battery, machine gun bn., engineer bns., pioneer bn., signals, medical, veterinary and ordnance units, pay section, mounted troops, cyclist company, supply column and ammunition park.

Light Horse Bdes.
1st Bde.: 1st, 2nd, 3rd Rgts. *2nd Bde.:* 5th, 6th, 7th Rgts. *3rd Bde.:* 8th, 9th, 10th Rgts. *4th Bde.:* 4th, 11th, 12th Rgts. *5th Bde.:* 14th, 15th Rgts.

The Light Horse had their own machine gun squadrons, field ambulances and veterinary sections.

Australian Corps units
Artillery, heavy artillery, heavy trench mortar battery, tunnelling companies, railway operating companies, mechanical transport companies.

Camel Corps with supporting units.

An Australian carries his wounded mate down from the hills for treatment at Anzac Cove, without getting himself parted from his rifle. Bayonets were almost invariably kept fixed at Anzac: base areas did not exist, in the normal sense, and danger was ever-present. (Australian War Memorial)

Mk III SMLE, with its 17-inch bayonet. It was to prove its rugged worth from the sands of Palestine to the mud of Flanders.

After consultation with the governments of Australia and New Zealand, Kitchener formed the antipodean contingents into an improvised Australian and New Zealand Army Corps; the initials of this formation, stamped onto stores as ANZAC, became the most famous word in Australian and New Zealand army history. Its commander was Lieut. General Sir William Birdwood.

The AIF's first major operation was the landing at Gallipoli on 25 April 1915. The object was to take control of the Dardanelles, the narrow strait linking the Aegean Sea with the Black Sea[1]. Command of the expedition was given to Gen. Sir Ian Hamilton, who faced a daunting task.

[1] See the present writer's *Damn the Dardanelles*, Osprey, 1980.

The Gallipoli peninsula has four sets of beaches – at Bulair at the neck, Suvla Bay, Ari Burnu and at the tip, Helles. Its mountainous spine is scarred with deep ravines and gullies.

The Australians and New Zealanders were sent in to a dawn landing at Ari Burnu, but the first assault force, the Australian 3rd Brigade, was landed a mile too far north, at what was soon known as Anzac Cove. A Turkish flare went up and soon a hail of bullets was spattering the shallows and striking sparks from stones on the beach. The boats grounded and the Australians jumped over the gunwales and splashed to the beach. Some were hit; others went in out of their depth and were dragged under by their heavy kit.

The troops faced almost perpendicular cliffs under which companies and platoons were jumbled in confusion. Junior officers quickly rallied the troops and within minutes a rough line of about six companies was clawing its way up the slopes. Some men moved far and fast. By 7am a young officer and two men had climbed three ridges and were looking down on the object of the whole operation, the Narrows, only three and a half miles away. Another party was halfway up Chunuk Bair, a dominating peak around which 50,000 men would be killed during the campaign.

As much furious fighting occurred on 25 April in the wild country around Anzac Cove as in any battle in history. No front line existed, and men landing later in the day were just as vulnerable to enemy bullets as men in the gullies inland.

Their first bayonet rush carried the Australians to a hill known as Baby 700, but incessant enemy fire made the position untenable. By nightfall the Anzacs held a position about two miles long by three-quarters of a mile deep. On Hamilton's orders they burrowed, hacked and tunnelled into the seaward slopes of the ridges. For three days after the landing the fighting was savage, with wave after wave of Turks making frontal attacks on the Anzac lines.

By 1 May reinforcements were required. The only available forces were the Light Horse regiments in Egypt. Despite the value of the Light Horse in the defence of Egypt, the enthusiasm of the brigades to fight, even without their beloved horses, finally influenced Hamilton to employ the Light Horsemen in a dismounted rôle, but they served intact in their regimental and brigade groups.

The only grenades the Anzacs had were jam tins filled with explosive, nails, stones, pieces of glass and shell shards, so they became adept at catching the Turkish 'cricket-ball' grenades and throwing them back.

On the night of 18–19 May the Turks put 42,000 men into a massive attack on the Anzac position, where Gen. Birdwood had only 12,500 front line men. They killed thousands of Turks in the attack, and the first hour was sheer slaughter. At daybreak the Turkish officers gave up all efforts to lead, and drove their men into the Anzac fire. Australian reserves came pushing into the line, even offering to pay other men to make room for a place on the parapet. Later in the campaign Anzacs offered as much as £5 for the 'privilege' of getting an unofficial place in a bayonet charge. When the Turks broke off the action at midday they had lost 10,000 men; 5,000 of these, dead and wounded, lay in the open in No Man's Land.

The Australians' physical appearance impressed all visitors to Anzac. Compton Mackenzie, the novelist, then on HQ staff, wrote: 'They were glorious young men. Their almost complete nudity, their tallness and majestic simplicity of line, their rose-brown flesh burnt by the sun and purged of all grossness by the ordeal through which they were passing, all these united to create something as near to absolute beauty as I shall hope ever to see in this world.'

But even 'glorious young men' are mortal. In fighting at Lone Pine, in August, six Australian battalions lost 80 officers and 2,197 men. Battalions of the 1st Brigade lost most heavily, and few witnesses of outstanding bravery remained. Consequently, of the seven Victoria Crosses awarded after this fight, four went to a reinforcing battalion, the 7th. In that fierce month two Light Horse units, the 8th and 10th, were practically wiped out.

Nowhere on the peninsula could the British and French make any significant progress; and eventually evacuation became inevitable. At Anzac Cove it was brilliantly planned by Lieut. Col. Brudenell White of the Anzac Staff. More than 83,000 men with horses, guns and some supplies were moved out in the period 10–19 December, with only two soldiers wounded in the final stages of the evacuation. The Australians left behind 7,594 killed; Gallipoli had cost them an additional 19,367 wounded.

The Light Horse were reinforced and re-organised; during 1916–1918 they fought 36 battles between the Suez Canal Zone and Damascus, in Syria, as well as many small actions. The Australian horsemen were men of resolution and resource, accustomed to responsibility, and equally to strong sunshine and dusty roads. They chafed under collective discipline, but every man was self-disciplined. For this reason the Light Horse never wasted a bullet; one historian has claimed that the Light Horse-

One of the most famous soldiers of the 1st AIF was Pte. John Simpson Kirkpatrick of 3rd Australian Field Ambulance. At great risk he used a donkey, 'Murphy', to evacuate wounded down the steep, exposed slopes to beach dressing stations; and he was eventually killed during one of these missions of mercy, on 19 May 1915. He is commemorated in a sculpture by W. Leslie Bowles. (Australian War Memorial)

A characteristic group of Australians on a General Service wagon passing through a French village near Amiens in 1916–17. Note the formation sign painted on the side of the wagon bed just behind the front wheel – cf. Plate H. (Australian War Memorial)

men probably fired fewer wild shots than any other combatants of the war.

The 150 tired young veterans of the 39th had battle of Romani, fought on 3–5 August 1916. Chauvel knew that the Turks, striking for the Suez Canal, could not afford to leave the little tableland of Romani menacing their flank. He had only about 1,600 dismounted rifles against a much larger enemy force, and his thin line covered three and a half miles. 'Allah! Allah! Finish Australia! Finish Australia!' the Turks yelled as they attacked. But the Light Horsemen held firm against infantry, machine gun and artillery attack for 24 hours. At dawn next morning Chauvel counter-attacked with his outnumbered, exhausted and thirsty troopers, and swept the Turks before him. By midnight on 5 August the Turks had suffered 5,350 casualties and another 4,000 had been taken prisoner. The Battle of Romani was the decisive engagement of

the Sinai-Palestine campaign; before Romani, British strategy and tactics were defensive, the stand of the 1st and 2nd Light Horse Brigades reversed the situation. The Turks never regained the initiative.

An even more spectacular action took place during the battle of Beersheba. The conflict had reached the point where Chauvel had to be in possession before nightfall on 31 October 1917 or give the Turks a chance to reinforce their garrison. He sent the 4th Light Horse Brigade, under Brig. Gen. Grant, in a hell-for-leather charge against infantry in prepared positions. The 4th and 12th L.H. Regiments formed up in three lines from 300 to 500 yards apart, with bayonets in hand in lieu of sabres. The Turks opened fire on the galloping horsemen but few were hit. The lines of troopers cleared the first Turkish trenches at a bound and charged the main line, four feet wide and ten feet deep. The whole operation took about an hour; 38 Turkish officers and 700 other ranks were captured, as well as nine field-guns, three machine guns and great quantities of supplies and transport. Some

Light Horse brigades were later issued with swords so that charges could be more effectively driven home. The news of Grant's charge swept through Palestine, and Gen. Allenby later spoke of the Light Horse as 'the spirit' of his army.

Spirit was also needed on the Western Front. On 14 July 1916 the three divisions of the 1 Anzac Corps – the 1st, 2nd and 4th – were concentrated in the area west of the Amiens-Doullens road. The flank of the British Fourth Army, engaged in the great Somme battles, was held up by the stubborn German defence of a key village, Poziéres. Lieut. Gen. H. B. Walker was ordered to take Poziéres with the 1st Australian Division, and the battle began on 23 July on a one-mile front, with two brigades forward and one in reserve. The Diggers went in close behind their own artillery fire. An officer of the 6th Field Artillery brought a gun to within 200 yards of an important German trench and devastated the defenders with 115 rounds at point-blank range. Throughout the ruins of Poziéres that morning the Australians played a grim sport – 'ratting'. They rolled phosphorus bombs into cellars and dugouts to flush out snipers and machine gunners. Terrified, the Germans then fled, only to be chased and bayoneted or shot. Then the Australians would squat on another doorstep, to have a quiet smoke and wait for other victims. Another sport was 'prospecting' – looking for trouble or prisoners just for the fun of it.

Right from the beginning the Australians adopted their own peculiar attitude to shellfire. By common unspoken agreement they ignored it. No matter what duty they happened to be engaged on, they stood upright and walked casually through the barrage; they refused to crawl and often did not turn their heads.

The fighting at Poziéres was ferocious. In a 13-hour battle on 26 July the men of the 17th Battalion threw 15,000 grenades. No front trench could be maintained for more than a day before bombardment filled it in. So great was the carnage in the 24th Battalion that months afterwards, even when the battalion's positions had been obliterated, their course could be traced by half-buried bodies with the red and white patches of the battalion showing on their arms.

In a single tour of duty at Poziéres the Diggers

Capt. Albert Jacka, VC, MC and Bar. This officer was awarded the supreme decoration for gallantry at Anzac when serving with the 14th Bn.; it was generally believed in the AIF that he merited a second VC for an action in France. (**Australian War Memorial**)

said they were under a greater stress than during the whole of the Gallipoli campaign. Having captured the ridge, one of the only two advances on the whole of the British front, they had to hold it. Shelling so pulverised the front that Lieut. Col. Ray Leane, bringing up his 48th Battalion, could not even find the front-line garrison's trenches. Leane was the most famous fighting commander of the first AIF. A stern, virile man with a keen sense of duty and honour, Leane had so many relatives in his battalion that the AIF knew it as the 'Joan of Arc Battalion' (Made of All-Leanes . . .).

The 4th Division bore the brunt of the German counter-attacks for nine days, yet in six successive night attacks they brought the British line to within striking distance of the key point of Mouquet Farm. The three divisions' final casualty figures for Poziéres were: 1st Division, 7,700; 2nd Division, 8,100; 4th Division, 7,100. This was a

A surgeon captain attending a wounded man in an Australian Advanced Dressing Station during the fighting at Hill 60, Ypres, on 26 August 1917. (Australian War Memorial)

rate of one man in three. It has been said that Poziéres Ridge is 'more densely sown with Australian sacrifice than any place on earth'.

Australian divisions were almost constantly in the line in France and Belgium. All five took part in the Passchendaele (Ypres) Offensive of October-November 1917; at one time four Anzac divisions attacked side by side, the only occasion on which that has ever happened.

An officer of the 3rd Machine Gun Company wrote one of the most famous orders of the war, while commanding a section at Messines, a particularly dangerous place on the Ypres front. It ran:

Special Orders No. 1 Section 13/3/18

(1) This position will be held, and the Section will remain here until relieved.

(2) The enemy cannot be allowed to interfere with this programme.

(3) If the Section cannot remain here alive it will remain here dead, but in any case it will remain here.

(4) Should any man through shell shock or other cause attempt to surrender, he will remain here dead.

(5) Should all guns be blown out the Section will use Mills Grenades and other novelties.

(6) Finally, the position, as stated, will be held.

F. P. Bethune, Lt.

O/C No. 1 Section.

The Australians' most successful operation was the capture of Mont St Quentin, the 'Gibraltar of the Somme', 30 August–3 September 1918. In a copybook operation, Gen. Sir John Monash captured the German bastion in what was possibly the finest single feat of the war. His battalions overcame scores of well-sited machine gun nests on a long, gradual slope through the initiative of section leaders backed by individual dash. Mont St Quentin, Sir Arthur Conan Doyle said, was 'a supreme object lesson of that individual intelligence and character which have made the Australian soldier what he is'.

But this reputation was won at great price. Of the 332,000 Australian troops who embarked to fight in the distant theatres of the First World War, 212,773 became casualties, including 53,993 killed or died of wounds or gas. Australian casualties, in proportion to the number of troops embarked for overseas service, were the highest of any country engaged in the war. This was because the great majority of the Australians were front-line soldiers. Only 140,000 Diggers were discharged fit.

The 'Young' Diggers – 1939-45

In the first year after demobilisation, 1920, the Australian militia numbered 100,000 – all compulsorily enlisted men born in 1899, 1900 and 1901. There was a cadre of 3,150 permanent officers and men, about 150 more than in 1914.

Because of motorisation some changes were dramatic; in 1937 four Light Horse regiments became machine gun regiments, equipped with Vickers .303s and a strange variety of trucks. (But they kept their emu plumes!) By 1938 the permanent army had shrunk to 2,795 and the citizen army to 42,895, but in the wake of war scares in Europe it shot up to 70,000 in March 1939 and to 80,000 by the outbreak of war, September 1939.

Australia entered the war with problems entirely different from those of the First World War. Two land forces were required, one for service overseas and one for home defence. Accordingly, a second AIF was raised by voluntary enlistment for service abroad, and by compulsory service a militia force was created for home defence.

Following the 1st AIF tradition (1st, 2nd, 3rd, 4th and 5th Divisions) the 2nd AIF commenced with the 6th Division and followed with the 7th,

8th and 9th. The 6th, 7th and 9th were sent to the Middle East and later to the Pacific. The 8th went to Malaya, on Japan's entry into the war, and was captured there.

Each of a division's three infantry brigades at the beginning of the war had four battalions, not three as in the new British Army. Because of this and other differences between British and Australian organisation the establishment of the 6th Division was 16,528, which was 3,336 more than that of a British division.

It was necessary to organise a division in which quotas of all arms were provided by each State. This was done by following closely the organisation of the 1st Division of the 1st AIF. Thus the 16th Brigade, like the 1st Brigade of 1914, consisted of four battalions raised in New South Wales, the 2nd/1st, 2nd/2nd, 2nd/3rd and 2nd/4th. The prefix 2/ distinguished them from the 'ordinary' 1st, 2nd, 3rd and 4th Battalions, which were among the NSW battalions of the militia which had inherited Battle Honours of the corresponding units of the old AIF. Even in units

Sir John Monash, the able commander of the AIF in France, bestows a decoration on a soldier, whose side view clearly shows the voluminous cut of the Australian tunic. Its skirt pocket usually bulged with ammunition, grenades, and a wide assortment of unofficial kit. (Australian War Memorial)

A tableau of uniforms in the Australian War Memorial, Canberra. From left to right: Infantryman in desert uniform, with a neck-cloth added to the peaked cap; the pith-helmet was considered, but was unpopular with Australians. Left centre is a lieutenant of Light Horse, and behind him a mounted trooper in full marching order. At right is a cavalry staff officer, with scarlet armband.

where no corresponding unit existed in the 1st AIF, as in anti-tank regiments, the prefix 2/ was used to avoid confusion with militia units.

Beyond the system of numbering and the coloured shoulder patch no effective link was established between the AIF and the home militia army, with unhappy results that lasted to the end of the war. So high was the prestige of the volunteer AIF that a desire to qualify for membership in its brotherhood and to march on Anzac Day was a strong motive for enlistment.

Pay was not a major incentive. At the beginning of the war an unmarried private received five shillings a day, with an additional two shillings a day deferred pay after embarkation. An additional three shillings a day was paid to married men, and one shilling for each child. The AIF men often referred to the militia derisively as 'Chocolate Soldiers' or 'Chokos', but the militiamen proved their mettle in helping to turn the Japanese tide of invasion in New Guinea, at Milne Bay and in the Owen Stanley Ranges.

Each AIF battalion had a headquarters company of six platoons (signals, mortar, carrier, pioneer, anti-aircraft and transport and administrative) and four rifle companies each of three platoons, each of three sections. Every section had a Bren light machine gun, a 2 in. mortar and, depending on the war area, a Boys anti-tank rifle. The mortar platoon was armed with two 3 in. mortars, and the carrier platoon with ten Universal carriers armed with Brens.

Another innovation was the division's mechanised carrier regiment, equipped with 48 carriers and 28 light tanks; the carriers were armed with a Bren and a Boys, the tanks with a heavy and a medium machine gun. Artillery regiments consisted of two 12-gun batteries of 25-pdrs. The division also had an anti-tank regiment, equipped with 2-pdrs. To carry its heavy equipment, stores and ammunition each division had 3,163 vehicles.

The standard small-arm of the Australian soldier during the Second World War was the No. 1 Mk III* SMLE; this differed from the earlier version in that the magazine cut-off, long range dial sights and windage equipment on the rearsight were omitted. Later in the war the long bayonet gave way to the spike bayonet. The lighter-weight No. 5 jungle carbine version was also issued to some extent in the Pacific.

The 6th Division reached the Middle East early in 1941. Its officers had been well chosen from the regular officer corps and the militia, and its senior officers had been outstanding leaders in the Australian Corps in France in 1918. The Commander-in-Chief was Gen. Sir Thomas Blamey. The 6th had been in training for nearly a year when it was sent against the Italians in Libya. The Australians fought their first battle at Bardia on 3 January 1941. The men were heavily clad with greatcoats and leather jerkins over their uniforms, and laden with weapons, tools, ammunition, grenades and three days' rations. In an astonishingly successful action the division captured 40,000 Italians, 960 guns, 130 tanks, 700 trucks and huge quantities of war material. In this first British victory of the Second World War, the 6th Division lost 130 men killed and 326 wounded. Later that month the division captured Tobruk and a further 27,000 prisoners for a loss to themselves of 49 killed. In six weeks they chased the Italian Army for 740 miles across Egypt and Libya, and broke it.

The 9th Division and a brigade of the 7th garrisoned Tobruk – to begin one of the great military defence sagas and to inflict on the Germans their first land defeat of the war. Under Maj. Gen. Leslie Morshead the Australians held the coastal fortress against all that Rommel could throw against them. The last unit out was the 2/13th Battalion, evacuated 242 days after the siege began. The Australians lost 1,000 men during the siege but took more than 2,000 prisoners – a large number for a besieged garrison to capture.

The 6th Division, meanwhile, had been in action in Greece and Crete. A 'scratch army' of Greeks, Australians, British and New Zealand troops fought bitterly against a massive German armoured onslaught supported by dive-bombers, but were driven back. Evacuated to Crete, 6,500 Australians and 7,700 New Zealanders fought several separate battles, this time against German paratroops and glider-borne soldiers, in a defence

The Australian War Memorial tableau includes this cameleer of the 1st (Anzac) Bn., Imperial Camel Corps, formed in Egypt in 1916; in all, four battalions were raised. The uniform differed from that of the Light Horse in that puttees replaced leggings, and ostrich plumes were not issue. The shoulder patch was a red triangle.

which began on 19 May 1941. On 27 May, at Suda Bay, the 2/27th Battalion (Lieut. Col. T. G. Walker), helped by men of the New Zealand Maori Battalion, made a bayonet charge of 600 yards. It demoralised the Germans and sent them running. In a broadcast over Radio Berlin, Col. Erhard Loehter said: 'Our boys thought the Australians would not take a bayonet charge seriously because they smiled so broadly . . . we are no longer deceived by these obliging grimaces.'

The campaign ended with a long, arduous evacuation march across Crete by thousands of mixed troops. Throughout 27–28 May a spirited rearguard action was fought from Suda to Sfakia, where many men were taken off. While the Royal Navy carried out its desperately dangerous evacuation the highly disciplined 2/7th Battalion gallantly held the beach perimeter, and had to be left behind. More than 3,000 Australians were captured in Crete; but the German casualties were so heavy that they never again attempted a major airborne operation.

With British fortunes at a low ebb, it was decided to invade Syria and Lebanon, held by

Order of Battle
Second A.I.F. 1939–45

6th Division
16th Bde.: 2/1st, 2/2nd, 2/3rd Bns.
17th Bde.: 2/5th, 2/6th, 2/7th Bns.
19th Bde.: 2/4th, 2/8th, 2/11th Bns.

7th Division
18th Bde.: 2/9th, 2/1st, 2/12th Bns.
21st Bde.: 2/14th, 2/16th, 2/27th Bns.
25th Bde.: 2/25th, 2/31st, 2/33rd Bns.

8th Division
22nd Bde.: 2/18th, 2/19th, 2/20th Bns.
23rd Bde.: 2/21st, 2/22nd, 2/40th Bns.
27th Bde.: 2/26th, 2/29th, 2/30th Bns.

9th Division
20th Bde.: 2/13th, 2/15th, 2/17th Bns.
24th Bde.: 2(28th, 2/32nd, 2/43rd Bns.
26th Bde.: 2/23rd, 2/24th, 2/48th Bns.

Each division had its own cavalry (armour), artillery, engineers, signals, service corps, medical corps and provost company.

Non-divisional units: eight Independent Companies and 11 Commando Squadrons.

1 Australian Corps Troops: 2/1st, 2/2nd, 2/3rd, 2/4th Machine Gun Bns. 2/1st, 2/2nd, 2/3rd, 2/4th Pioneer Bns.

Australians of the Imperial Camel Corps near Rafah, Palestine, in January 1918. The cameleers, nearly all of them former Light Horse troopers, were used for long-range desert patrols and raids, some of them spectacular.

the pro-German Vichy French commander, Gen. Dentz, with 28,000 French and African troops and about 10,000 Lebanese and Syrians. The British GOC could spare only two brigades of Australians – the 21st and 25th Brigades of the 7th Division; the 5th Indian Brigade; and some Free French troops. The field commander was Lieut. Gen. J. D. Lavarack. Among the many steps taken to conceal the invasion plan was an order to the Australians within sight of the enemy not to wear their slouch hats; they had to wear caps, pith helmets or steel helmets. Any indication of the feared Australians preparing for action, it was believed, would stir the enemy into a frenzy of activity: the reputation of the Light Horsemen who had fought in this area in the First World War was still vividly remembered.

The invasion began on 8 June, in summer heat and among harsh, rocky hills much more easily defended than captured. But it was also good country for Australian unorthodoxy and daring. The 2/31st Battalion (Lieut. Col. S. H. Porter) made an arduous night journey in trucks along the winding road to Jezzine, which they captured next evening in a dashing attack.

Commanders encountered places where the use of tracked vehicles on a narrow path was impossible. In this emergency the Kelly Gang (named after Australia's most notorious bush-ranger) came into being. It comprised 40 horsemen, mostly former Light Horsemen, and it performed valuable patrolling service in the hill regions of Lebanon and Syria.

Some units of the 6th Division, notably the 2/3rd Battalion, were sent to reinforce the 7th Division brigades. The 2/3rd, in a fine attack, scaled rocky hills overlooking Damascus and captured several forts from the French Foreign Legion. A detached company cut the Beirut-Damascus road, then climbed up the sheer face of a gorge and took a fort. Another 2/3rd company, in a daring night attack, even captured the daunting and dominating mountain of Jebel Mazar. By such spirited actions the Australians forced the surrender of Damascus on 21 June.

Dentz sought an armistice, and fighting ceased on 12 July. The hard-fought campaign had cost the Australians 1,600 casualties, including 416 killed.

Sgt. Tom Derrick, VC, DCM, of 2/48th Bn.; note that he also wears the Africa Star with 8th Army cypher. Derrick won his DCM at Tel-el-Eisa, Libya, in July 1942, and his VC for extraordinary gallantry at Satelberg, New Guinea, on 23 November 1943. Later commissioned, he declined to accept a training appointment, and was killed in action in Borneo in 1944. The details of 2nd AIF uniform are clearly seen here: the buttons bearing the map of Australia, the 'rising sun' collar badge, the 'Australia' shoulder title, and the 'colour patch' at the top of the sleeve. This shoulder patch displays all the elements of design: the T-shape, identifying the 9th Division and referring to its service in Tobruk; the light grey outer rim or base, signifying the 2nd AIF; the light blue inner rim, indicating the division's 26th Brigade; and the white centre, identifying the 2/48th Bn. (Australian War Memorial)

The Australian Army's service in the Middle East ended spectacularly with the 9th Division, under Gen. Morshead, acting as the spearhead of Gen. Montgomery's offensive at El Alamein on 23 October 1942. On the right of the battle line, astride the coastal road on which the major pursuit must follow any breakthrough, the 9th had the vital rôle. The official British report on the battle stated: 'The 9th Australian Division put up a magnificent effort. They fought themselves and the enemy to a standstill, till flesh and blood could stand no more. Then they went on fighting.' In fact, they fought for 12 days. In later years Field Marshal Montgomery told the

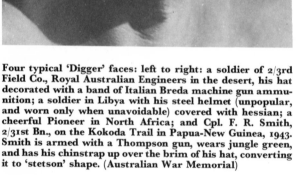

Four typical 'Digger' faces: left to right: a soldier of 2/3rd Field Co., Royal Australian Engineers in the desert, his hat decorated with a band of Italian Breda machine gun ammunition; a soldier in Libya with his steel helmet (unpopular, and worn only when unavoidable) covered with hessian; a cheerful Pioneer in North Africa; and Cpl. F. R. Smith, 2/31st Bn., on the Kokoda Trail in Papua-New Guinea, 1943. Smith is armed with a Thompson gun, wears jungle green, and has his chinstrap up over the brim of his hat, converting it to 'stetson' shape. (Australian War Memorial)

present writer that his plan 'depended' on the Australians 'crumbling' the Germans holding the strongest part of the Axis line. The 9th's losses between 23 October and 4 November were 2,694, including 620 dead. For the whole period of the Alamein operations losses were 5,809, including 1,225 dead.

Meanwhile the 6th and 7th Divisions had returned to Australia to fight in the Pacific campaign. Since the Japanese had taken Singapore Australia was vulnerable, and the seasoned AIF units were needed in the New Guinea jungles. Gen. Blamey was recalled to command the Australian Military Forces (AMF), which were a mixture of AIF and militia units.

The first and greatest jungle operation was the Battle for the Kokoda Trail, which crossed the high, mountainous spine of Papua-New Guinea. Sometimes called the Battle of the Ranges, it lasted seven months, resulted in defeat for the Japanese Army, and ended the myth of Japanese infantry invincibility.

Lightly-defended New Britain and New Ireland had fallen quickly. In New Guinea the Japanese objective was the capital, Port Moresby, the supply link with Australia. Until the 6th and 7th Divisions could be brought in, the defence of Papua-New Guinea depended on militia battalions. With some outstanding exceptions, these units had low morale.

A formation known as 'Maroubra Force' commanded by Lieut. Col. W. T. Owen was trying to stem the Japanese thrust. The striking unit of this 'force' consisted of one grossly understrength battalion, the 39th, formed of a few hundred militiamen stiffened by AIF reinforcements. Their average age was 18. If the Japanese could break them and take Kokoda airfield, the only means by which the defenders could receive adequate reinforcement and supplies, they would be in Port Moresby before the AIF could arrive.

The battle was to be fought in jungles, swamps and mountains and in a dreadful climate. The whole Owen Stanley Range, which reaches a height of 13,000 feet, is a maze of ridges, spurs, valleys and rivers. Much fighting took place on a one-man front – the width of the track. Many Australians were killed or wounded by snipers who tied themselves into position high up in trees, and waited to pick off an officer or NCO. For this reason the Australians abandoned badges of rank and nobody was addressed by rank; even senior officers were known by a codename, so that a CO might be 'Dick' or 'Curly'.

After several aggressive rearguard actions Col. Owen's battered battalion was forced back. When the leading Japanese troops met opposition they deployed and engaged while support troops moved in with machine guns and mortars. To defend the vital position of Kokoda Col. Owen had about 80 men in all, including 60 young infantrymen.

That night, 26 August, 500 Japanese attacked. In this first pitched battle on Papuan soil attackers and defenders became mingled in the confused fighting. Col. Owen was mortally wounded in an ambush, and for several days the 39th fought a gallant rearguard action under Maj. Alan Cameron. With malaria and dysentery adding to their casualties, the battalion was in poor shape by the time it reached Isurava. Here what was left of Maroubra Force was taken over by an AIF veteran officer, Lieut. Col. Ralph Honner, who had been ordered hurriedly to the crumbling front. Honner decided on a stand at Isurava. He had only a few hundred men and his largest weapons were 3in. mortars firing a 10lb shell. Pressing him were three battalions of a Japanese regiment, with another full regiment coming up fast. Supporting them were a mountain artillery battalion and two engineer units – about 4,000 in all.

Despite these odds, for two weeks the Australians fought the Japanese hand-to-hand in a series of ambushes and raids. One group of 39th sick and wounded were on their way down the trail to Moresby when, hearing that the battalion was fighting to survive, they disobeyed orders, turned round and hurried back into action.

Infantrymen of the 2/17th Bn., 9th Division, photographed at Tobruk in 1941 serving a captured Italian 75mm gun; the self-styled 'Bush Artillery' proved highly effective during the siege. (Australian War Memorial)

On 28 August Maj. Gen. Horii, the Japanese commander, launched a full-scale offensive. Five battalions of Japanese, shouting their 'Banzai' war-cry, made frontal attacks on Australian positions. Horii did not then know it but he was too late to win the campaign. He was now facing the AIF.

The 150 tired, young veterans of the 39th had left Isurava the day before the battle, fighting their way out down the trail. The Japanese were now up against the first AIF battalion to reach the battle – the 2/14th, soon joined by part of the 2/16th, both of the 21st Brigade. On 30 August, General Horii concentrated his battalions in a narrow valley for a decisive blow against the still heavily-outnumbered Australians. On the entire 350-yard Australian front he laid down a storm of artillery shells, mortar bombs and continuous machine gun fire; then wave after wave of infantry went in. The veteran Australians beat back every assault. One platoon repulsed 11 attacks, each of 100 or more men. This platoon, losing its commander and all NCOs, was then led by a private soldier, with other privates acting as NCOs.

The Australians held Isurava for four days before Japanese weight became too great. The Australian commander, Brig. Potts, could not challenge Horii's control of the upper spurs and ridges without weakening the defence of the main track, the Australians' lifeline and the way to Moresby. The 2/14th and 2/16th Battalions made a slow, deliberate withdrawal. A bloody bayonet charge checked the Japanese, but their outflanking movements isolated parties of Australians, and those captured were killed on the spot.

At Iora Creek an ever-thinning line of Australians killed 170 Japanese and kept their line intact before withdrawing to Imita Ridge, the last defensible point of the Owen Stanleys. Here they held while the Japanese dug in on the facing ridge, Iorabaiwa. Horii had a chance to smash through, but again he was too late. The three battalions of a fresh AIF brigade, the 25th (Brig. Eather), relieved the exhausted 21st Brigade. Eather was ordered to die on Imita Ridge rather than withdraw.

While the Japanese were striking for Port Moresby, a linked action was developing at Milne Bay 200 miles to the east, where the 7th Infantry Brigade, militia, and 18th Infantry Brigade, AIF – both under Maj. Gen. C. A. Clowes – were defending vital airfields. By 7 September, after much patrol fighting, the Japanese had lost the battle and at least 1,000 dead, mostly élite marine assault troops. Milne Bay was the first clear-cut land victory against the Japanese anywhere in the war.

In the Owen Stanleys the 25th Brigade, using the Australian-made Owen gun – a light sub-machine gun for close-quarter fighting – soon dominated the valley between Imita and Iora-baiwa ridges. For the first time the Australians had artillery – two 25-pdrs dragged painfully up the tracks. On 26 September General Horii began a withdrawal. From Kokoda the Australian infantry pushed on steadily. At Gorari on 11 November the 2/25th and 2/31st battalions made fierce bayonet charges, killing 580 enemy in fighting that lasted five days. Ten weeks later the last bitter phase of the battle was fought at Buna, Sanananda and Gona in a vast morass of swamp, mud and devastated jungle.

The Australians fought many jungle campaigns over the next 30 months in New Guinea, Borneo, New Britain, the Solomon Islands and other parts of the Pacific; they made amphibious combat landings at Salamaua, Tarakan, Wewak, Labuan, Brunei and Balikpapan. The fighting was necessarily borne by the infantry; armour was little use in swamp and jungle, and artillery had a limited rôle. When the war ended the Australian Army had lost 18,713 men killed in action.

Korea, Malaya, Borneo and Vietnam

In keeping with Australian tradition, demobilisation began immediately the war against Japan ended and within a year was almost completed. Three battalions were raised for service with the British Commonwealth Occupation Forces in Japan. An armoured car squadron and an Australian general hospital were also sent. In 1948 the three battalions were redesignated the 1st, 2nd and 3rd Battalions, Australian Regiment. They became the Royal Australian Regiment (RAR) the following year.

These three battalions were the nucleus of Australia's post-1945 army and its first regular field force for immediate action in a national emergency. To augment this force the Citizens Military Force (CMF), with its roots in the old pre-1939 militia, was re-formed in 1948. National service training was introduced in 1951 and continued for eight years.

In 1950 North Korean troops crossed into South Korea, which appealed to the United Nations for help. Australia was one of the first member-states to promise aid. The 3rd Battalion RAR, then in Japan, was in action by September of that year.

One of the most spectacular Australian victories was at Sariwon, 'the Aldershot of North Korea'. It was clear that a conventional attempt to capture this stronghold would be bloody and probably abortive; so two company commanders of the 3rd Battalion, Majors G. M. Thirlwell and I. B. Ferguson, worked a bluff. They mounted a tank with an interpreter and had themselves driven towards the enemy. They told the North Koreans that they were surrounded and heavily outnumbered and suggested that they surrender. After tense hesitation 1,982 enemy surrendered with quantities of anti-tank guns, machine guns and mortars.

The 3rd Battalion could also fight conventionally; in one action on 22/23 October 1950 they made a bayonet charge in which they killed 270 North Koreans and captured 239, at a cost to themselves of seven wounded.

The origin and development of the Australian 'rising sun' badge is one of the most interesting aspects of Australian military history.

Appropriately enough, it began with a collector, a major in the South Australian forces, who thought of the design to mount his collection of bayonets. He asked a captain in the South Australian navy to help him build a trophy-shield, using timber and brass.

This shield seems to have come into the possession of Gen. Sir Edward Hutton, who was appointed to command the military forces of the new Commonwealth of Australia. The trophy of arms, fixed above his office door, comprised a semi-circular red-painted board, on which bayonets and sword-bayonets were arranged alternately, surrounding a crown cut from sheet brass. Specifically the weapons were the Martini-Henry rifle triangular socket bayonet and the cut-and-thrust sword-bayonet.

In 1902 when the 1st Battalion Australian Commonwealth Horse was being raised for service in the South African War the GOC apparently decided on a general service badge and suggested 'something like' the trophy of arms. The contingent was due to leave five days later and a first badge was hurriedly struck. It consisted of seven triangular points above 'AUSTRALIA' and the crown on a form of wreath base.

This design was amended for later contingents, with six intermediate points between the larger ones. The metal around 'AUSTRALIA' was pierced, probably to sew a piece of coloured cloth beneath. Still later that year another variation was struck with 'COMMONWEALTH HORSE' forming the badge's base; it was worn by Australian troops who went to London for the coronation of King Edward VII.

It is possible that the badge designers were symbolically including the six-pointed Commonwealth Star, which is the major part of the crest of Australia. The origin of the 'rising sun' title given to the badge is connected neither with the sun, nor heraldry, nor history, but with a brand of jam. Until about 1906 the only building near Victoria Barracks, Melbourne, was Hoadley's jam factory, which produced a widely advertised 'Rising Sun' brand; large quantities were shipped to the Australians in South Africa, and the jam's trademark was striking. In Melbourne returning soldiers were sometimes called 'Hoadley's Horse'.

In 1903 the badgemakers J. R. Gaunt & Son of Birmingham designed a badge whose basis did not change until the 1970s. The inscription on the scroll was 'AUSTRALIAN COMMONWEALTH MILITARY FORCES' until 1949 when it became 'AUSTRALIAN MILITARY FORCES'. In the 1970s it was shortened simply to 'AUSTRALIA' and minor changes were made in design.

After the much bigger battle of Kapyong, 24–25 April 1951, the 3rd Battalion received a US Presidential citation (with 2nd Battalion Princess Patricia's Canadian Light Infantry, and 'A' Company, 72nd US Heavy Tank Battalion). The citation read: 'The seriousness of the enemy breakthrough had been changed from defeat to victory by the gallant stand of these courageous soldiers . . . They displayed such gallantry, determination and *esprit de corps* in accomplishing their mission as to set them apart from and above other units in the campaign, and by their achievements they have brought distinguished credit to themselves, their homelands, and all freedom-loving nations.'

On the Imjin River front, in October 1951, the 3rd Battalion was heavily involved in attacks on Hills 317 and 217. That on 5 October on Hill 317, a key point in the Chinese winter line, was as fierce as anything in Australian military experience. The hill was pyramid-shaped and so steep that it could be climbed only on hands and knees. From their apparently impregnable positions the Chinese tried to smother the attack with heavy machine gun fire. But the Australians, with supporting artillery fire and air-strikes just ahead of them, inched their way forward. As dusk fell they clawed their way onto the plateau and in a bayonet-charge routed the Chinese, who left 68 dead. On Hill 217 the battalion withstood repeated counter-attacks throughout the night of 8/9 October, and again the Chinese withdrew, leaving 120 dead.

In 37 months all three regular battalions saw service in Korea and added new honours to an already impressive reputation. By the time the armistice was signed in 1953, 278 Australian soldiers had been killed in action.

The 'Malayan Emergency' had begun in June 1948 and lasted 12 years. Australian troops, already committed to Korea, were not sent to Malaya until 1955. As in Korea, the force consisted of volunteer regular soldiers. Their task for five years was the unpublicised but exhausting one of patrolling the 'pacified' areas. When the Emergency ended in 1960 15 Australians had been killed and 27 wounded.

Despite the end of the Emergency there was still fighting in the area. The proposal to form a

1. Mounted Infantryman, South Africa, 1900
2. Major, NSW Lancers, c.1900

A

1. Trooper, 4th Light Horse; Palestine, 1917
2. Private, 7th Bn.,AIF; Gallipoli, August 1915
3. Private, AIF; Gallipoli, 1915

B

1. Sergeant, 27th Bn., 7th Bde.,2nd Div.,AIF; Europe, 1918
2. Sergeant, Field Artillery, 3rd Div.,AIF; Europe, 1918
3. Company Sergeant Major, 1st MG Bn., 1st Div.,AIF; Europe, 1918

C

1. Private, 2/13th Bn., 7th Div.; Tobruk, 1941
2. Corporal, 2/1st Bn., 6th Div.; N.Africa, 1941-42
3. Captain, 2/14th Bn., 7th Div.; N.Africa, 1941-42

1. Sergeant, 2/31st Bn., 25th Bde., 7th Div.; Papua-New Guinea, 1941-42
2. Infantryman, Papua-New Guinea, 1943-44
3. Commando, Independent Companies; Pacific islands, 1944

E

1. Major, 8th Royal Australian Regt., late 1960s
2. Private, Royal Australian Infantry, 1970s
3. Private, 5th Royal Australian Regt.; Vietnam, 1966

F

1. Lieutenant-Colonel, Royal Australian Regt. of Artillery, 1970s
2. Cadet Colour-Sergeant, RMC Duntroon, 1970s
3. Corporal, 3rd Royal Australian Regt., 1970s

1

3

2

4

5 6 7

8 9 10

11

12

13

14

15

16

17

18

19

20 21

22

23

24

25 26 27

28 29 30

31 32 33

34

35

36

37

38

39

H

Federation of Malaysia provoked Indonesia into what it called 'Konfrontasi', a word taken into commonwealth military history as 'Confrontation'. In April 1963 Australian troops from the Far East Strategic Reserve helped defend Borneo against Indonesian guerrillas raiding Sabah and Sarawak. The 3rd and 4th Battalions, RAR, with their own artillery and engineering support, were responsible from 1963 for a front of 35 miles to a depth of 30 miles – a particularly exacting form of warfare. The Australian task was defensive: to prevent Indonesian troops from infiltrating. The whole campaign was largely one of jungle patrols and scouting, with occasional clashes on the trails. In a debilitating climate the work called for physical and mental toughness of a high order.

While Australian units were involved with Confrontation the Vietnam situation was rapidly deteriorating. The first Australians to serve in that theatre were 30 highly experienced soldiers formed into the Australian Army Training Team and posted to Vietnam in July 1962 to help South Vietnamese units. Three years later the Australian Government committed a task force of three battalions with support arms and services. The Australians operated in Phuoc Tuy Province, south-east of Saigon, a difficult jungle area.

The first of four VCs in Vietnam was awarded to Warrant Officer K. A. Wheatley for an example of courage typical in Australian forces since the Boer War. Wheatley, of the Australian Army Training Team, went out with a Vietnamese company on 13 November 1965, on a search-and-destroy mission. Accompanied by Warrant Officer Swanton, he was in the right platoon, which came under Viet Cong fire in open rice fields. Wheatley radioed that Swanton had been hit and asked for an air-strike and aircraft to evacuate casualties. His platoon of Vietnamese began to break under fire; the medical orderly told Wheatley that Swanton was dying, and then ran. Refusing to abandon Swanton, Wheatley half dragged and half carried him towards the jungle 250 yards away. As the Viet Cong came running through the jungle Wheatley pulled the pins from two grenades and calmly awaited the enemy. Soon afterwards came two grenade explosions and

The bronze 'Australia' shoulder title was worn only by the 1st and 2nd AIF – that is, by men who had enlisted voluntarily and had volunteered for overseas service. The upper 'colour patch' on this captain's tunic is a miniature in yellow and purple, signifying First World War service in the 30th Bn.; the lower Second World War patch is full size, its rectangular shape indicating 6th Division, the grey edge the 2nd AIF, and the brown-over-red central bars the 2/7th Bn. (Philip Katcher)

several bursts of fire. The two Australian bodies were found next morning. Wheatley had obeyed the Australian concept of 'mateship'.

The most important Australian battle in Vietnam took place at Long Tan in August 1966, when the 108 men of 'D' Company, 6th Battalion RAR (Maj. H. Smith) advanced into a Viet Cong trap set by at least 2,500 men. Under almost blinding tropical rain two platoons moved through a gloomy rubber plantation – into the sudden onslaught of mortar and small-arms fire. Sheltering behind tree trunks and in hastily scratched pits, the Australians drew together into a circle and faced the surrounding enemy. Coolly, they stopped wave after wave of suicidal enemy attackers. But their own ammunition was run-

Walking wounded in New Guinea, 1943. The US Army webbing gaiters were much more practical in the jungle than the short British anklets. The Australian soldier's three identity discs are worn by the left hand man, and all three carry labels specifying the treatment received at the Advance Dressing Station. They are Privates W. H. Walker, K. E. Beckmann and B. R. Chadwick, all Militiamen. (Australian War Memorial)

Wounded on their way out of the line during the Pacific campaign. Seriously wounded were evacuated on stretchers carried by New Guinea natives, affectionately known to the soldiers as 'fuzzy-wuzzy angels', from their huge heads of hair. (Australian War Memorial)

ning low and a supporting air-strike was impossible. The battalion's CO, Lieut. Col. Townsend, led 'A' Company in an attack on the enemy rear. After three hours the Viet Cong broke and ran, carrying some dead and wounded. They left behind them 245 dead and they suffered probably 350 wounded. The Australians lost 17 dead and 21 wounded.

The Australian Army Aviation Corps was established in 1968 and quickly built up a reputation in Vietnam, flying observation, reconnaissance, surveillance and medical evacuation missions. The Corps is equipped with the Bell 206B helicopter, the Australian twin-engine Nomad light aircraft, and the single-engine Pilatus Porter light observation plane.

The Australian Army Training Team, whose strength had grown to more than 200, had been the first unit into Vietnam and it was the last one out, in December 1972. It was by far the most distinguished Australian unit in Vietnam, winning four Victoria Crosses, the American Meri-

torious Unit Citation, the Vietnamese Gallantry Citation and many personal awards for bravery. Vietnam was Australia's longest war – well over ten years. No war in which Australia has taken part aroused such violent political reaction, for and against participation.

About 47,000 soldiers served in Vietnam, many of them for two and even three 12-month tours. At its peak of commitment Australia had 8,000 troops in Vietnam. Casualties were 415 killed and 2,348 wounded.

The Australian approach to warfare in Vietnam was completely different from that of the Americans. The Americans usually preceded their infantry attacks with massive aerial bombing; but whether they did this or not they would then move through the jungle in large, close-knit groups, often noisily, hoping to defeat any ambush

A Warrant Officer Class 1 of the 2/1st Bn. gives bayonet-fighting instruction to a section of Potential Officers at an infantry warfare school near Sydney, 1942. The white puggaree and scrubbed gaiters were worn only by men who had returned from overseas service, although the short khaki puttees did not necessarily signify lack of such service. (Australian War Memorial)

by superior fire-power. The bombing often sent the Viet Cong scurrying, undefeated, out of an area. Often the Americans did not see or hear the enemy, who slipped away from advancing patrols until they could themselves strike with maximum impact. The Australians fought this war in the way that the 2nd AIF and the militia divisions had fought the Japanese. Their small patrols spread out and moved quietly through the jungle; if one man encountered the enemy his mates would close in rapidly to attack them from all sides. Their success proved the Australian methods to be the best. In the words of Brig. T. F. Serong of the Australian Army Training Team: 'Conventional soldiers think of the jungle as being full of lurking enemies. Under our system, *we* do the lurking.'

Some Australians in Vietnam used the 'riot' shotgun. Because of their mutilating effect such guns are prohibited by the Geneva Convention, hence their use only in undeclared wars, such as that in Vietnam. The more general weapon was the M16 (Armalite), which was still being issued to some units in 1975.

The Australian Special Air Service fought in Indonesia and Vietnam. It is not regarded as an élite force (as is the British SAS), simply as a specialist one. With great experience of modern war it is designed to gain maximum information from limited resources and to help in the application of 'economy of force'. An example of their successful technique was shown in Vietnam. Over a period of six weeks six SAS patrols carried out constant surveillance over 15,000 metres of enemy approaches to the Australian base. Twice-daily reports by these patrols kept the command continually informed, thus enabling the whole force to take part in a large-scale sweep without being worried about having an open flank. Only one infantry company was left behind for base defence. An SAS patrol in Vietnam could operate for 14 days on its own supplies. This endurance enabled the SAS to move slowly and stealthily deep into enemy territory, where they found that the Viet Cong tended to be noisy and careless when they considered themselves secure in their base areas. SAS patrols penetrated Viet Cong base areas, made close reconnaissance and sprung ambushes with devastating surprise; they killed at least 500 Viet Cong for the loss of one Australian. When Gen. William Westmoreland commanded Allied forces in Vietnam he ordered a training school, based on ASAS methods, for Americans and other troops.

The operations in Vietnam carried out by the Centurion tanks of the Royal Australian Armoured Corps were also notably successful, and involved interesting tactical innovations. For space reasons they are not included here, but are described and illustrated in detail in Vanguard 22 *The Centurion Tank in Battle*, Osprey, 1981.

By February 1974 all but 600 Australian soldiers had returned to Australia from the nation's commitments in Singapore and Malaysia, and after April 1975 only 150 were left as instructors, and advisers. Infantry companies go in rotation to Butterworth, Malaysia, for three months' tropical training – Australia's only troops overseas at the time of writing.

Since the Second World War the Australian Army has had four major re-organisations – 1957, 1960, 1964 and 1973. In 1957 a Regular Army strength of 21,000 was established, including a brigade group of 4,200. The 1960 re-organisation was mainly because of changing combat conditions in South-East Asia; the one-army concept (CMF/Regular) was developed. In 1964 the Army's Field Force was changed to provide divisions with more infantry battalions and to give more flexibility to their deployment.

Also in 1964 the Government re-introduced

Badly wounded Digger of 3rd Bn., Royal Australian Regiment receiving field treatment in Korea, 1952–53. (Australian War Memorial)

29

National Service in an attempt to increase the Regular Army's field force. At the start ballot-selected 20-year-olds served for two years full-time, then for three years in the Reserve. In 1972 call-up for National Service ended after a change of government.

The most significant re-organisation took place in 1973. This involved the rationalisation of senior Army commands and control systems. The old geographic commands were replaced by three functional commands – Field Force Command, Training Command and Logistics Command, plus military districts in each state. Each command has Australia-wide responsibilities.

In 1974 the CMF was re-organised to make it a more effective and viable force in Australian defence. Renamed the Australian Army Reserve, it trains and operates alongside professional soldiers of the regular army.

Weapons

The SMLE Mk III* had been used from the Second World War to Korea as the standard infantry weapon, and nearly 400,000 were manufactured at Lithgow up to 1956. Throughout the 1970s the Army's weapons were chosen on the basis of much field experience in South-East Asia. The soldier's rifle is the LIAI Self-Loading Rifle (SLR), a 7.62mm lightweight, semi-automatic with an effective battle range of 300 metres (the Belgian-designed FAL). The light machine gun is the L4A4, and the general-purpose machine gun is the heavier M60. Many ranks carry a 9mm Browning automatic pistol. Another main weapon carried by the infantry is the claymore mine; weighing only 1.5kg, it is an effective anti-personnel device at 100 metres.

Australian infantry are equipped with several anti-armour weapons, principally a very close-range weapon, the No. 94 Energa grenade; it is fired from the SLR using a ballastite cartridge. A more familiar weapon is the one-man 66mm Rocket Light Anti-Tank Weapon, the first of the recoilless weapons and much used in Vietnam. Other weapons are the 84mm Gun Anti-Tank Carl Gustav (Medium Anti-Tank Weapon) and the M40A1 106mm, another medium-range weapon.

Until the 1980s the artillery's main weapons were the 105mm howitzer and the 140mm (5.5in.) medium gun. There are two types of howitzer: one, a heavy weapon towed by a vehicle, fires a 14.9kg (33lb) shell over a distance of 11,000m. The largest gun of the Australian artillery is the 5.5in. medium gun, firing a 36.3kg (80lb) shell over 17,000m. The junior branch of artillery, air defence, is equipped with shoulder-fired Redeye missiles and the trailer-mounted Rapier.

The Plates

A1: Private, Australian volunteer mounted infantry; South Africa, 1900
This soldier of a Bushmen's unit is dressed in a simple uniform of khaki drill, without insignia. The two-pocket tunic has a stand collar, normally worn open and sometimes with a knotted handkerchief or sweat-rag. The breeches are confined by puttees wound from the top, tied at the ankle – the opposite practice to 1914–18. The slouch hat has a plain khaki puggaree, a rolled length of cloth pressed flat and then wound with cord; the plumed ostrich feathers were still worn by Light Horse personnel in 1914–18. The weapon is the .303 Magazine Lee Enfield Mk I*; on the march it was carried with the butt in a 'bucket' by the right stirrup, and the trooper rode with his hand on it at all times so that he could 'take it with him' if he fell off. Ammunition is carried in a 50-round bandolier, each section of ten individual loops having a flap fastened by two brass studs. A haversack and canteen are slung on the left side. The saddlery is standard apart from the bridle, which is unique: it is the standard headroller with a local pattern of bit buckled on by a short strap. The trooper's blanket, a horse rug and fodder are all carried. The Bushmen's horses were all taken to the war from Australia, being of higher quality than any brought from England or found in South Africa.

A2: Major, New South Wales Lancers, 1897–early 1900s
The hat badge is an elephant's head with crossed lances and a wreath, the collar badge the tusked

Note that this private of the 3rd Royal Australians in Korea, 1953, still carries the venerable SMLE Mk III, essentially the same weapon as the Gallipoli Anzacs. The white tapes in the background aided night movement round the company area; and note the sandbagged 'hoochie' or field kitchen. (Australian War Memorial)

elephant's head alone, both being in white metal. The ranking on the red shoulder strap is gilt. Note whistle lanyard just visible at throat; and unique pattern of sword frog, designed for this élite corps of the State of New South Wales – see photo earlier in this book showing mounted sergeant-major. The hat plume is of glossy cock's feathers.

B1 : Trooper, 4th Light Horse Regt.; Palestine, 1917
This regiment distinguished itself in a famous charge at Beersheba, in which they held their bayonets in lieu of sabres. This, and other figures on Plates B and C, wear the first pattern of service tunic which was made of drab serge, cord or heavy flannel; the original light drab colour faded in time to reveal the colour of the material before dyeing, either neutral or blue-grey. The light-and-dark-blue regimental 'colour patch' is worn at the shoulder. The leather gaiters or leggings are distinctively Australian. Personal

31

equipment includes a cavalry-pattern 90-round bandolier, and a further 50 rounds in pouches on the waist belt; and a water canteen with cavalry pattern mess-tin attached. The saddlery is standard British issue, with a string fringe added to the brow-band to keep off flies – a common practice in the Middle East.

A member of 'D' Co., 8th RAR photographed in Phuoc Tuy Province, South Vietnam. Normal section armament was the American M16 for the scouts, the SLR for the rest of the riflemen, and the American M60 for the gun group. Personal equipment tended to be worn according to personal preference, and was of mixed origin – some British, some US Army. A frequent 'set' would be two British '44 pattern pouches worn well behind the hips, so as not to risk injury if throwing oneself down in a hurry; two canteens on the back of the belt, perhaps with one or two British '56 pattern 'kydney' pouches; no shoulder braces; and the US rucksack-type pack. Grenades and M60 belts were liberally draped around most personnel in the field. (Australian War Memorial)

B2: Private, 7th Battalion AIF; Gallipoli, August 1915
The battalion is identified by the brown-over-red patch at the shoulder of the drab flannel tunic. Dressed for the Lone Pine assault, this Digger wears quick-identification field signs in the form of white calico armbands and a white patch on his back.

B3: Private, AIF; Gallipoli, 1915
The most famous non-uniform in the world – 'Gallipoli undress', worn behind the battle line. Ready to hand is the Digger's rifle and bayonet (with unmodified quillon, typically Australian at that date) and ammunition belt. By late summer 1915 most Anzacs were gaunt from dysentery and exhaustion. Typically, this soldier has been collecting British regimental badges as souvenirs. The pennies at the left recall the Australian soldier's favourite gambling game, 'Two-Up': the coins are tossed, and bets taken as to whether they will come down both 'heads' or both 'tails'.

C1: Sergeant, 27th Bn., 7th Bde., 2nd Australian Division; Europe, 1918
This NCO, having a 'cuppa' with two mates at a refreshment stall on a London railway station on the way back to the Western Front, wears Field Service Marching Order. The brass 'A' on his brown-over-blue battalion 'colour patch' identifies a veteran of Gallipoli. The rank chevrons on the khaki serge tunic are in the 'cross-hatch' pattern typical of that period, and still to be seen occasionally in the AIF of 1940, in contrast to the normal British pattern made up of herringbone or 'arrowhead' threads. He also wears, on the right forearm only, four blue overseas service chevrons, one for each year.

C2: Sergeant, Field Artillery, 3rd Australian Division; Europe, 1918
This NCO, in walking-out dress, wears the bandolier, breeches and leggings typical of mounted troops. Unlike the other figures he wears the drab flannel tunic, now fading to its original blue-grey shade. Like the other figures he wears the bronze shoulder title 'Australia', and the sun-burst badge on both collar points and – just visible here – on the normally up-turned left

Soldiers of the Royal Regiment of Australian Artillery in winter service dress (ceremonial) for an inspection during the 1970s. Note that the escorting officer wears above the right breast pocket both the US and the South Vietnamese unit citation ribbons. (Australian Army)

brim of his slouch hat. The rank chevrons are worn on the right arm only. On the left forearm is a vertical gold wound stripe, and on the left breast the ribbon of the Military Medal. The shoulder patches are in the oval shape of this division, and in traditional artillery red and blue.

C3: Company Sergeant-Major, 1st Machine Gun Bn., 1st Australian Division; Europe, 1918
This Warrant Officer wears ribbons not uncommon in the First World War: the Military Cross (open to WOs as well as to officers), the Distinguished Conduct Medal, and the Military Medal. The crossed brass machine guns worn below the rectangular unit shoulder patch are distinctively Australian. Just visible on the right forearm are four overseas service chevrons below the crown of this rank, and on the left forearm two gold

A corporal (left) wearing winter service dress (ceremonial), displaying the uniform of basically British appearance, with corps or unit badges on the hat and collar, which replaced the earlier battledress uniform in the 1960s. Lanyards in unit colours are worn on the right by most of the Army, but on the left by the Royal Australian Regiment. (Centre) is a major wearing officer's winter service dress, again with ceremonial additions in this photograph. (Right) is a corporal in the pale khaki drill shirt and shorts of tropical dress; the only 'ceremonial' embellishment here is the addition of full decorations. The green summer dress and khaki summer dress will be found on Plates F and G. (Australian Army)

wound stripes. The weapon is the Mk VI Webley .45in. revolver; note that unlike C1 this WO does not carry the bayonet, its scabbard strapped to the entrenching tool handle. The commodious pockets of the AIF service dress tunic could accommodate up to eight Mills grenades in all. The

confident stance of these men recalls the characteristic 'style' of the Australian soldier, much remarked upon by the rather more staid British.

Note that the basic shapes of unit 'colour patches' in the AIF were according to division: a flat rectangle for 1st Division, a diamond for 2nd, an oval for 3rd, a disc for 4th and an upright rectangle for 5th.

D1: Private, 2/13th Bn., 7th Australian Division; Tobruk, 1941

The slouch hat, greatcoat and weapon were essentially unchanged since the Great War. The personal equipment was now the British 1937 webbing set, scrubbed almost white in North

Africa. The pose recalls the fearsome reputation enjoyed in the desert by Australian troops, whose bayonet charges shook even battle-hardened German units. There was a rumour current among Italian personnel – a rumour apparently given wide credence among the less sophisticated – that Australians ate their prisoners . . . The basic shapes of the 'colour patches' of the 2nd AIF, always on a grey backing, were a flat rectangle for the 6th Division, a diamond for the 7th, an oval for the 8th and, initially, a disc for the 9th – this latter was changed to a squat 'T' to commemorate the siege of Tobruk from 1942. This figure wears the light-blue-over-dark-blue rectangle of the 2/13th Bn. superimposed on the 7th Division's diamond. The differences between the basic shapes and the shapes of the inner colour patches were due to an entirely pragmatic deployment of units to divisions.

D2: Corporal, 2/1st Bn., 6th Australian Division; North Africa, 1941–42
See Plate H for shoulder patch detail. Unlike most British troops, by now issued with the waist-length battledress blouse, the 2nd AIF units wore the thigh-length, four-pocket service tunic with the 'rising sun' badge on each collar and the 'Australia' title on the shoulder straps. The hessian-covered helmet and 1937 webbing are standard British issue. The weapon is the Boys .55 anti-tank rifle; like most weapons of this class it proved of very limited value against the battle tanks of the Second World War, but in the hands of Australians this powerful rifle was effective at knocking holes in enemy machine gun posts and the old Italian forts of Libya. The corporal rests it on a knocked-out German PzKpfw III tank.

D3: Captain, 2/14th Bn., 7th Australian Division; North Africa, 1941–42
Khaki drill tropical combat dress is worn with the familiar 'Digger' hat, in this case adorned with Cellophane anti-gas goggles (worn as protection against blowing sand), and the 'colour patch' of the 2/14th Bn. on the puggaree – yellow over dark blue on the division's diamond backing. Standard British-style cloth ranking, in cream and brown thread on red infantry backing, is worn on slip-on

loops on the shoulder straps above a woven 'Australia' title. Standard webbing pistol set is arranged for personal comfort, with the issue .38in. Smith & Wesson reversed on the left hip, and water-bottle and binocular case worn here on the right. In common with most British troops, the Aussies usually managed to 'lose' their respirator cases by 1942.

E1: Sergeant, 2/31st Bn., 25th Bde., 7th Australian Division; Papua-New Guinea, 1941–42
This figure, based upon contemporary photographs of the author, wears combat dress typical of the Kokoda Trail fighting. The 2/31st Bn. killed more than 500 Japanese at the battle of Gorari, the fiercest bayonet charge of the Pacific War. Uniforms were roughly dyed green (from khaki drill) while on the troopships going to New Guinea, and variations were common. The US Army webbing gaiter was standard issue. The hat bears the battalion 'colour patch', a horizontally divided black-over-red disc, on the right of the puggaree, and the AIF sunburst

The modern combat uniform of the Australian infantryman, less rucksack-style pack and US-type steel helmet; cf. Plate F2. The weapon is the 7.62mm SLR, semi-automatic, with 20-round magazine. (Australian Army)

badge in bronze on the left brim. No badges of rank were worn in the jungle, as they attracted the attentions of Japanese snipers. Many troops were issued with the standard '37 pattern utility pouches, but numbers still wore the smaller 'cartridge carrier' pouches on the belt; slung cotton bandoliers holding 50 extra rounds – two five-round clips in each of five pockets – were common.

E2: Infantryman, New Guinea, 1943–44

Steel helmets were not commonly worn on the Kokoda Trail, but were standard issue. This Bren gunner, crossing a jungle river, wears the same

uniform as the sergeant but with the legs of his trousers cut off for comfort; many photographs show this combination of shorts and long gaiters. Again like F1, he has a rolled groundsheet/rain cape on top of his pack. Note machete slung at the hip.

E3: Commando, Independent Company; Pacific islands, 1944

The slouch hat was seen as often as the official issue black beret of these commando companies. The trousers are the lower half of the US Army herringbone twill fatigues, widely issued to Australian troops; the long US Army gaiters have been cut down for convenience. Unofficial embellishments, common in the Pacific jungles, include in this case a yellow scarf, a lucky boar's tusk, and a number of grenade rings worn on the dog-tag cord. Weapons are a 'sawn-off' 1907

The pride of the Royal Australian Armoured Corps – the Australian version of the German Leopard (ASI) main battle tank. At 42 tons weight it has a range of 600 kilometres, a top speed of 62 km/h, and can snorkel through water 2.25m deep. The main armament is the 105mm, with a range of 8,000m. (Australian Army)

bayonet, Mills HE 36 grenades, and the 9mm Owen sub-machine gun. The excellent Australian-made Owen, with its 33-round box magazine mounted above the action, was one of the most unusual-looking weapons of the war; deceptively light and toy-like, it proved extremely effective and reliable in jungle fighting, and was still in use by some British and Commonwealth troops during the Malayan Emergency many years later.

F1: Major, 8th Royal Australian Regiment, late 1960s

The green summer ceremonial uniform. Note that the hat badge is now that of the Royal Australian Corps of Infantry, not the AIF 'sunburst'. Bronze rank insignia and 'RAR' cyphers are worn on the shoulder straps, and above the medals can be seen the bronze wreath-and-

bayonet Combat Infantry Badge. The left-shoulder lanyard is in the brown of 8th RAR; other battalion colours were blue (1st Bn.), black (2nd), green (3rd), maroon (7th), grey (9th), etc. Like many Australian officers this veteran came up through the ranks. His decorations are the Distinguished Conduct Medal, British Korean War Medal, UN Korean Medal, General Service Medal with 'Malaya' clasp and oakleaf Mentioned in Despatches emblem, 1962 GSM with 'Borneo' and 'Vietnam' clasps, Australian Vietnam Medal with MiD oakleaf, and South Vietnamese medal for Australian troops.

The M113 APC; the infantry have only a few of these under command, most being operated by the RAAC or RACT and attached to infantry units at need. In Vietnam effective use was made of various modifications of the basic personnel carrier with support weapons turret-mounted on the roof, such as this T50 Cadillac-Gage turret mounting two machine guns, and the larger turret from the Saladin armoured car mounting a low-velocity 76mm gun. (Australian Army)

F2: Private, Royal Australian Infantry, 1970s

The combat version of the same uniform, with – in some photographs – camouflage-painted webbing equipment, and the US-style steel helmet. The weapon is the US M16A1 with grenade launcher. The first field dressing is taped to the left shoulder brace.

F3: Infantryman, 5th Royal Australian Regiment; Vietnam, 1966

See caption to photograph elsewhere in this book for comments on webbing equipment. The weapon is the US M60, and US grenades of various types are carried. A rolled groundsheet/rain cape would be tied below the rucksack. A camouflage-scrim face veil is worn as a scarf, and the face is streaked with black and brown greasepaint. The black gaiters, modelled on the US wartime style but fastened by two buckled straps, were distinctively Australian; they were replaced by high laced combat boots from the end of 1966. Insignia were not normally worn in the front line, but the yellow-on-drab-green 'sunburst' patch of Australian Forces Vietnam was sometimes seen. The British-style bush hat bore names and other decorations at personal or unit whim, and this cloth twist through the foliage loops is typical. (One platoon of 8th RAR wore a square patch of Macleod tartan on the back of the hat, in honour of the platoon commander's ancestral clan!)

G1: Lieutenant-Colonel, Royal Australian Regiment of Artillery, 1970s

A senior officer in 'patrol blues', the officers' full dress uniform. The Army parachute brevet is worn at the right shoulder, the Army AOP flying brevet on the left breast, ranking on the shoulder straps, and the RARA's corps badge on the cap band, with artillery 'grenades' on the collar. Decorations which might typically be worn are the MBE, DFC, British and UN Korea medals, 1962 GSM with clasps for Borneo and Vietnam, and Australian and South Vietnamese medals for Vietnam.

G2: Cadet Colour Sergeant, Royal Military College, Duntroon; 1970s

Founded in 1911, the RMC Duntroon is a degree-conferring institution; cadets are commissioned after completing a four-year course, but honour students remain for a fifth year. The RMC badge – crossed upright boomerangs and the motto 'Doctrina Vim Promovit' in a scroll – is worn at cap and collar. The colour sergeant's ranking is three gold chevrons beneath crossed Australian flags beneath a crown.

G3: Corporal, 3rd Royal Australian Regiment, 1970s

In summer khaki ceremonial uniform, this junior NCO wears chevrons of conventional herringbone pattern but smaller size than the British model. The regimental cypher is worn on both shoulder straps, the battalion's green lanyard on the left. Above the right pocket is the ribbon of the US Presidential Citation won by the 3rd RAR in the Korean War; above the left, the Combat Infantry Badge. The decorations are the Australian and South Vietnamese service medals for the Vietnam War. Note blackened, polished webbing belt. The weapon is the standard SLR (more exactly, L1A1).

Plate H: Insignia: see also comments under Plates C, D: 1914–18:

(**1**) Shoulder patch, 1st Bn., 1st Division, AIF, with brass 'A' for 'Anzac' signifying service at Gallipoli. (**2**) 2nd Div. HQ – the white-within-black was the normal combination for HQ troops. (**3**) 4th Div. Artillery. (**4**) 4th Bn., 1st Div. (**5**) 55th Bn., 5th Div. (**6**) 11th MG Coy., 3rd Div. (**7**) 5th Light Horse Regt. (**8**) 5th Pioneer Bn. (**9**) 4th Div. Supply Train. (**10**) 1st Div. Engineers. (**11**) 1st Div. vehicle sign. (**12**) Ribbon of proposed Anzac or Gallipoli Star, devised but never issued: the red was for the Army, the blue for the Navy, the yellow for the Australian wattle and the silver-grey for the New Zealand fern-leaf. (**13**) Shoulder title of 10th Bn., of type worn before issue of cloth shoulder patches in 1915. (**14**) Unofficial badge of Australian 1st, 3rd and 4th Bns., Imperial Camel Corps, 1916–18. (**15**) Badge of 5th Victoria Mounted Rifles, 1900, South African War. (**16**) Sunburst badge, pre-1949 pattern; as worn on turned-up left brim of hat, and in smaller presentation on collar. (**17**) Bronze shoulder title worn by 1st and 2nd AIF, denoting volunteers for overseas service.

(**18**) 2nd Anzac Corps vehicle sign, First World War. (**19**) Combat Infantry Badge, instituted 1970, awarded to serving members of the Army who have, since 1950, given 90 days' service as infantrymen during operations. (**20, 21**) Ribbons for the Australian Vietnam Service Medal and the South Vietnamese medal awarded to Australians. (**22**) Cloth shoulder title worn on battle-dress blouse in 1950s–60s. (**23**) Rank badge of Warrant Officer Class 1, worn on right sleeve of 'patrol blues'.

1939–45:
(**24**) 2/1st Bn., 6th Div. (**25**) 2/29th Bn., 8th Div. (**26**) 2/31st Bn., 7th Div. – an atypical example. The battalions of 25th Bde. – 2/25th, 2/31st, and 2/33rd – decided on their own patch designs while in England, and the round patch did not conform to the division's normal diamond shape. (**27**) 26th Bde. HQ, 7th Div. (**28**) 6th Div. Cavalry (armour). (**29**) 7th Div. Signals. (**30**) 2/24th Bn., 9th Div. (**31**) 6th Div. Medical Corps. (**32**) 8th Div. Artillery. (**33**) 2/1st MG Bn. – the triangle indicated troops under Army command; and cf. Plate C3. (**34**) 6th Div. vehicle sign. (**35**) Ribbon for Australia Service Medal, 1939–45.
(**36**) Badge of 3rd New South Wales Bushmen, raised in the Transvaal, South Africa, 1901. (**37**) Parachute brevet for Australian Special Air Service, post-1945. (**38**) Crossed rifles were the marksman's badge until after 1945; they then became the skill-at-arms badge, with an added 'R' (rifle), 'L' (light machine gun), 'C' (machine carbine), 'M' (machine gun) or 'P' (pistol). (**39**) The issue button for Australian Military Forces, Second World War and for a period thereafter.

A lieutenant-colonel of the RARA (see Plate G1) in 'patrol blues', the Australian officer's full dress uniform. (Australian Army)

Farbtafeln

A1: Einfache khakifarbene Tropenuniform ohne Abzeichen; die Straussenfederbüschel waren noch im 1914–18 er Krieg beliebt. Das Gewehr wurde mit seinem Kolben in einem Leder 'Eimer' am Steigbügel getragen und der Lauf zu jeglicher Zeit in der rechten Hand gehalten, so dass ein herunterfallender Reiter es mit sich nehmen kann. **A2:** Die Elitekorps der Streitkräfte von 'New South Wales' trugen diese volle Paradeuniform; der Entwurf der Säbelhalterung war einmalig. Die Offiziere trugen Büschel aus Hahnenfedern.

B1: Das frühere Muster der Dienstjacke war manchmal aus schwerem Flanell oder Serge hergestellt, die durch die Benutzung, von khakifarben zu einem dumpfen blaugrau verblichen. Das Schulterabzeichen ist in den Regimentsfarben; diese Einheit zeichnete sich durch einen berühmten Angriff gegen die Türken bei Beersheba aus, ihre Bajonetts anstelle der Säbel tragend. **B2:** Braun über rote Schulterabzeichen lassen das Bataillon erkennen. Die weissen Armbänder und das Abzeichen auf dem Jackenrücken wurden zur schnellen Erkennung für die Truppen getragen, die bei Lone Pine, Gallipoli kämpften. **B3:** Eine typischere Ausstattung für die Truppen in den Schützengräben von Gallipoli. Die zwei Pfennige (links) wurden in dem beliebten Wettspiel 'Two-Up' der 'Digger' benutzt.

C1: Das 'A' aus Messing am Schulterabzeichen lasst einen Gallipoli Veteranen erkennen; die Abzeichenform identifiziert die 2. Division; die Farben identifizieren das Bataillon. Kleine blaue Winkel am Vorderarm zeigen den Dienst in Übersee an, einen für jedes Jahr. **C2:** Alte Flanelljacke zu grau verblichen. Beachte das 'Sonnenaufgang' Abzeichen der Australian Imperial Force am linken Hutrand, gewöhnlicherweise hochgeschlagen, und am Kragen. **C3:** Die gekreuzten Maschinengewehre aus Messing, unterhalb des Schulterabzeichens der Einheit waren ein spezielle australische Besonderheit. Das Kronenabzeichen dieses Ranges ist auf dem rechten Vorderarm, über den Armwinkeln für den Dienst in Übersee; und goldene senkrechte Streifen am linken Vorderarm zeigen die Verwundungen an. Die Schulterabzeichen waren in Form eines flachen Rechtecks für die 1. Division, ein Rhombus für die 2., ein Oval für die 3., eine Scheibe für die 4. und ein aufrechtes Rechteck für die 5.

D1: Ausser dem 1937er britischen Gürtelzeug, hat sich seit dem 1914–18er Krieg wenig verändert. Das Bataillon trägt ein helluber dunkelblaues Rechteck auf einem grauen Rhombusabzeichen; dies war die letzte Einheit, die Tobruk nach der Belagerung von 1941 verlassen hat. Alle 2nd AIF Einheiten trugen Abzeichen mit grauem Untergroud, ein flaches Rechteck für die 6. Div., ein Rhombus für die 7., ein Oval für die 8. und zuerst eine Scheibe für die 9., die später zu einer T-Form überwechselte, um Tobruk zu gedenken. **D2:** Im Gegensatz zu britischen Truppen, trugen die Australier noch eine lange Jacke mit vier Taschen anstelle der 'Kampfuniform-Blousons'. Das .55 Panzerabwehrgewehr war unwirksam gegen Panzer, jedoch nützlich im Kampf gegen Ziele der Infanterie, wie Maschinengewehrpositionen. **D3:** Das Bataillonsabzeichen wird rechts am Hut getragen; das Rangabzeichen ist von normaler britischer Art, wenn in Hemdsärmeln, wurde es an einem entfernbaren Tuchring getragen.

E1: Grob grüngefärbte khakifarbene Tropenkleidung gab es in vielen Schattierungen, und die Gamaschen der US Armee waren Einheitsausgabe. Das schwarz über rote Bataillonsabzeichen am Hut ist eine Ausnahme zu der Regel divisioneller Formen. Im Djungel wurden keine Rangabzeichen getragen, um zur schnellen japanischen Scharfschützen anlocken. **E2:** Die Hosen wurden im Djungel oft abgeschnitten. Der Stahlhelm war nicht so popular wie der australische 'Buschhut'. **E3:** Die Hosen und die abgeschnittenen Gamaschen sind nach US-Type; das m-pistole ist die ausgezeichnete in Australien hergestellte 'Owen'. 'Buschhüte' waren ebenso üblich innerhalb dieser Kommandokomapnien wie die ausgegebene schwarze Baskenmütze.

F1: Sommerparadeuniform in grün. Bronzen Rangabzeichen und 'RAR' auf den Schulterklappen. Infanterie Kampfabzeichen an der linken Brust über den Orden und Bataillonstaljereep auf der linken Schulter. **F2:** Einige Fotos zeigen Gürtelzeug in Tarnfarben angemalt. **F3:** In Vietnam wurde eine Mischung von britischen und US Gürtelzeug und Waffen benutzt. Beachte das Schulterabzeichen der australischen Streitkräfte in Vietnam, ein gelber 'Sonnenaufgang' auf grün; und besondere australische Gamaschen, nach dem Jahr 1966 durch höhere Stiefel ersetzt.

G1, G2: 'Patrol blues', komplette Offiziersausgehuniform, von einem regulären Offizier und einem Offizierskadetten an der königlichen Militärakademie mit dem vorübergehenden Rang eines Unteroffiziers getragen. **G3:** Sommerparadeuniform in khaki. Orden für Vietnam, Infanterie-Kampfabzeichen, bataillonsfarbener Taljereep und auf der rechten Brust die 'US Presidential Citation' von der 3RAR in Korea gewonnen.

H: Abzeichen – siehe Untertitel in englischer Sprache für Identifikation.

Notes sur les planches en couleur

A1 Simple uniforme khaki, sans insigne; les plumes d'autruche étaient encore populaires en 1914–18. La crosse du fusil reposait dans un 'seau' près de l'étrier, la main droite tenant constamment le canon de façon à l'entrainer avec soi en cas de chute. **A2** Le corps d'élite des troupes de New South Wales portait ce grand uniforme. Le type de suspension du sabre était unique. Ils portaient des plumes de coq.

B1 Les premiers modèles de tuniques de service étaient parfois en serge ou en flanelle épaisse qui se décolorait à l'usage, de khaki a un bleu-gris terne. Pièce d'épaule aux couleurs du régiment. Cette unité se distingua lors d'une charge célèbre contre les Turcs à Beersheba, effectuée à la bayonnette au lieu de sabres. **B2** Pièces d'épaules marron-sur-rouge identifient le bataillon. Les brassards blancs et la pièce au dos de la tunique furent utilisés pour identifier rapidement les troupes engagées à Lone Pine, Gallipoli. **B3** Tenue plus habituelle pour les hommes des tranchées de Gallipoli. Les pièces de monnaie à gauche servaient aux paris du jeu favori de 'Digger', le 'Two-up'.

C1 Le 'A' de laiton sur la pièce d'épaule identifie un vétéran de Gallipoli et la forme de la pièce est celle de la 2ème Division; les couleurs sont celles du bataillon. Un chevron bleu clair sur l'avant-bras par année de service outremer. **C2** Vieille tunique de flanelle ayant tourné au gris. Insigne 'soleil levant' de l'Australian Imperial Force sur le bord gauche du chapeau, d'habitude relevé, ainsi que sur le col. **C3** Les mitrailleuses croisées en laiton, portées sous la pièce d'épaule d'unité, étaient typiquement australiennes. Le couronne de ce grade se trouve sur l'avant-bras droit au-dessus des chevrons de service, et les bandes verticales dorées sur l'avant-bras gauche indiquent les blessures. Les pièces d'épaules étaient un rectangle pour la 1ère Division, un losange pour la 2ème, un ovale pour la 3ème, un rond pour la 4ème et un rectangle vertical pour la 5ème.

D1 Sauf l'équipement britannique de 1937, en toile, il y a peu de changements depuis la guerre de 1914–18. Le bataillon porte un rectangle bleu-clair-sur-bleu-foncé sur fond de pièce grise en losange. Cette unité sortit en dernier de Tobrouk après le siège de 1941. Toutes les unités de la 2nd AIF portaient des pièces à fond gris: un rectangle pour la 6ème Division, losange pour la 7ème, ovale pour la 8ème. La 9ème eut d'abord un rond qu'on changea ensuite pour un 'T' en commémoration de Tobrouk. **D2** Contrairement aux Anglais, les Australiens portaient encore une tunique assez longue à quatre poches à la place d'une 'battledress'. Le fusil Boys .55 inefficace en tant qu'anti-tank mais utile contre des cibles d'infanterie telles que des nids de mitrailleuses. **D3** La pièce du bataillon est portée à la droite du chapeau. L'insigne de grade est de type très habituel anglais et porté sur une boucle de tissu, amovible, quand on est en bras de chemise.

E1 Le khaki-vert des tenues tropicales subissait de grandes variations de tons. Guètres de l'armée américaine, règlementaire. La pièce noire-sur-rouge de bataillon, au chapeau, était une exception à la règle des modèles de divisions. On ne portait pas d'insignes de grade dans la jungle car ils attiraient l'attention des tireurs japonais. **E2** Dans la jungle, les pantalons étaient souvent coupés courts. Le casque d'acier n'était pas aussi populaire que le chapeau australien, le 'bush-hat'. **E3** Les pantalons et les guètres courtes sont de modèle américain. La mitraillette est l'excellent modèle Owen, fabriqué en Australie. Les 'bush-hats' étaient autant portés par ces compagnies de commandos que le béret noir réglementaire.

F1 Uniforme d'été de cérémonie, en vert. Insigne de grade en bronze et 'RAR' sur les pattes d'épaules; insignes d'infanterie de combat sur la poitrine gauche au-dessus des médailles, et cordon du bataillon sur l'épaule gauche. **F2** Certaines photos montrent l'équipement en toile peint en camouflage. **F3** Un mélange d'équipement en toile et d'armes anglais et américains étaient utilisés au Vietnam. La pièce d'épaule des forces australiennes au Vietnam était un 'soleil levant' jaune sur fond vert. Les guètres typiquement australiennes furent remplacées par des bottes plus hautes après 1966.

G1, G2 La grande tenue d'officier, 'Patrol blues', portée par un officier et un cadet de la Royal Military Academy, avec le grade temporaire de sergent. **G3** Tenue de cérémonie d'été khakie. Médailles du Vietnam, insigne de l'infanterie de combat, cordon aux couleurs du bataillon. Sur la poitrine droite, la citation présidentielle des USA, attribuée au 3ème RAR en Corée.

H Insignes Pour identification, voir les légendes en Anglais.